Allergies

Other Books by the Silversteins

Allergies

by Dr. Alvin Silverstein
and Virginia B. Silverstein

With an Introduction by
Sheldon G. Cohen, M.D.,
Consulting Editor

8537

616.9

S

Blairsville Junior High School
Blairsville, Pennsylvania

J. B. Lippincott Company / Philadelphia and New York

Photographs in this book have been provided through the courtesy of the following: Allergy Foundation of America, 21, 42, 44, 58, 59, 79, 101, 107, 110. Carolina Biological Supply Company, 46, 76, 81, 84; illustration pg. 76 © 1968 Carolina Biological Supply Company. Dr. John T. Connell, 38, 96. Carlos Crosbie, 61. Charles Hays and *Medical World News*, 23. McGovern Allergy Clinic, 98. Merck and Company, Inc., 90. *Science*, 121. Smith Kline & French Laboratories, 114. The photograph on page 12 is by the authors. Drawings on pages 50 and 54 are by Jean Krulis.

U.S. Library of Congress Cataloging in Publication Data

Silverstein, Alvin.
    Allergies.

    Includes index.
    SUMMARY: Explains the various types of allergies, their symptoms, causes, and treatment, and discusses research being conducted to find cures for allergic diseases.
    1. Allergy—Juvenile literature. [1. Allergy] I. Silverstein, Virginia B., joint author. II. Title. [DNLM: 1. Hypersensitivity WD300 S587a] RC584.S54   616.9'7   77-1284
    ISBN-0-397-31758-1   ISBN-0-397-31759-X (pbk.)

For Anne and Gerald Schoenstadt

Acknowledgments

The authors would like to thank the Allergy Foundation of America and others who kindly provided information. Special thanks to Dr. Sheldon G. Cohen for his careful reading of the manuscript and his many helpful comments and suggestions.

Contents

Introduction

Allergy gives rise to problems not only for the affected but also for the many who are concerned with its social and economic effects—family interrelationships, school absenteeism, days lost from work, the need to deal with environmental factors and the ever-increasing number of allergenic products emerging from modern technologies. No longer are we justified in underestimating the annoyance of an itch, a sneeze, a cough or wheeze; the risk of progression to ensuing disabilities is all too apparent. This special aspect of the story of allergy certainly extends the need to be informed far beyond medical specialists to those whose lives, occupations, and avocations are affected by the sensitizers and the sensitized—the patient and his parents, schoolteacher, and employer, the naturalist and the industrial worker. Additionally, if we are to include those who are daily exposed to potential allergens, who is not?

Especially relevant is childhood allergic illness, a situation where early detection and diagnosis that facilitate appropriate measures of prevention and treatment can offer the best opportunities to beneficially influence this group of disorders while still in early and reversible stages. To the writers, then, clearly and succinctly explain reasons and means for meeting these objectives, who give encouragement and directive thinking to the allergic person, who help to promote understanding and to shorten the distance between physician and patient—to Dr. Alvin and Virginia Silverstein—acknowledgement and appreciation are due. Their underlying message that team effort is required should not be lost, for the work of a physician is immeasurably advanced by the understanding of an enlightened allergic patient. While readers will find many points of interest, useful and helpful, to which they can personally relate, it may be pertinent to specially note two of these. First is the evident sense of accomplishment as the practice of allergy evolved to its present state of an established medical specialty scientifically based on an appreciation of immunologic mechanisms. Second is the authors' presentation of some material that must still be regarded in the area of concept and that will require definitive evidence before it is accepted as fact. However, the pace of our advancing knowledge in allergy is rapid. Some of the very problems being attacked by researchers, such as those highlighted in the authors' sampling, could well be solved or perhaps given different slants by new experimental leads even as this text is being read. Such is the nature of the field of allergy, where continuing progress resulting from the interactions of research scientists and clinical allergists, the effective application of biomedical data from the laboratory to health care, and anticipated rewards for the allergic patient are clearly visualized.

Sheldon G. Cohen, M.D.
Director
Immunology, Allergic and
    Immunologic Diseases Program
National Institute of Allergy
    and Infectious Diseases
National Institutes of Health
Bethesda, Maryland

Allergies

The August that Marianne was six, she suddenly began to sniffle and sneeze and rub her eyes. Her parents thought she had caught a "summer cold," but it wasn't an ordinary cold. There was no fever, and the "cold" just didn't seem to go away. Weeks went by, but Marianne continued to sneeze, and her eyes were itchy and watery. Then, one frosty day at the end of September, Marianne felt fine again. She had a few colds during the winter, but otherwise Marianne was a healthy little girl—until the middle of August, when the runny nose and eyes and sneezing fits started all over again. After a series of tests, Marianne's doctor told her parents that she was suffering from hay fever.

Jason had longed for a dog for as long as he could remember. One Christmas morning, he found an adorable cocker spaniel puppy waiting for him under the Christmas tree. What fun they had playing together. Jason didn't even mind the chores of feeding the puppy and cleaning up after it. The puppy followed him everywhere all day, and sometimes at night he would sneak it into his bed. They would

cuddle together, with the puppy licking Jason's face. But then one night Jason woke up frightened. It seemed as though he couldn't breathe. He gasped and cried. When his parents came to see what was wrong, they were alarmed. Jason was pale and sweaty, and he made a funny wheezing noise when he breathed. After a little while Jason felt better, and the family went back to sleep. But the next day, as he was playing with his puppy, he had another wheezing attack. And a few nights later he had another attack—such a bad one that his parents had to rush him to the emergency room at the hospital. The doctors gave Jason an injection and told his parents that he was suffering from asthma.

Betsy has always had to be extra careful about what she eats. She is allergic to wheat; whenever she eats anything containing wheat grain, she breaks out in hives—itchy, swollen lumps—all over her body. She can't eat ordinary bread or crackers, cookies or cakes, or noodles. She reads the labels carefully on all the foods she buys and politely turns down any foods she isn't sure of when she eats out. Yet Betsy's problems are simple compared to Ralph's —after twenty years of working in a bakery, Ralph developed a grain allergy. Just breathing the air when the dough was being mixed was enough to start him coughing and wheezing. He eventually had to quit his job and learn a new trade.

Lori was picking raspberries in the field near her house when a bee stung her. It wasn't the first time she had ever been stung, and she started home to get some first aid for the angry red swelling on her arm. But this bee sting was different. As Lori reached the house, she suddenly felt really sick. She began to vomit, and then felt that she could not breathe. She collapsed on the steps, unconscious. Her mother rushed her to the doctor, and they were just in time.

Without an injection of Adrenalin, Lori might have died.

Marianne, Jason, Betsy, Ralph, Lori, and millions of other allergy sufferers have one thing in common: their bodies react in an unusual way to substances that do not cause most people any difficulties. In some people, microscopic grains of pollen carried on the breeze, bits of household dust, the dander (skin particles) from animals, chemicals in foods and drugs, or the venom of an insect sting may trigger the body's defenses. Like firemen responding to a false alarm, the body reactions that normally protect us from invading germs and other threats are mobilized by these harmless substances. And "innocent bystanders"—the body's own tissues—may be hurt.

Medical specialists estimate that more than 35 million Americans suffer from allergies, ranging from the annoying sniffling and sneezing of hay fever to the life-threatening reaction that may result from an insect sting or an injection of a drug such as penicillin. If we include minor allergies such as the occasional skin rashes people may get from eating too much of a particular food or from contact with a particular fabric or detergent, then as much as half the population may be allergic.

Allergies can kill. About forty Americans die

each year from insect stings and bites, and about two thousand die from asthma. (The asthma toll is actually even higher, since asthma victims may develop heart disease or serious infectious diseases like pneumonia.) The typical allergy victim, however, is in little danger of dying. But he or she faces a lifetime of minor miseries —sniffles and itches and doing without, avoiding certain foods, arranging vacations to escape the pollen season, perhaps giving up a beloved pet or having to change jobs. Medical treatments are often a long process, and drugs may have annoying side effects. Allergies are the number one chronic disease among children. Fortunately, some allergies disappear as a person gets older; others may last a whole lifetime.

For a long time allergy was a sort of "stepchild" of medicine. Not too many doctors knew much about it or considered it very important. Even those who were aware of the widespread and varied problems of allergy felt frustrated. We knew so little about why some people sneeze when they breathe in grass pollen and others do not, why milk gives some people diarrhea and is a healthful and nourishing food for others. There seemed to be so little that could be done for many allergy sufferers.

But even though allergy has not received as much attention from researchers as it should, progress has been made. In science, advances in one field may provide clues to puzzles in other areas. Discoveries in various fields of biology and medicine have helped to bring new insights into allergy. The tools and techniques of the growing field of immunology, the study of the body's defenses, have been especially powerful. Scientists are now beginning to understand how the mechanisms of allergy work and to devise ingenious new ways of controlling them. Hope for the millions of allergy sufferers is growing.

Since Ancient Times

Though we are only now beginning to understand what causes allergies, people have been breathing air filled with pollen and mold spores, eating a variety of foods, living with animals, and getting stung by insects for many thousands of years. It is not surprising that many shrewd observers have noted that some people react strangely to these common things.

One of the earliest records of a description of allergies dates back to 3000 B.C., nearly five thousand years ago. The emperor of China, Shen Nung, ordered that pregnant women should not eat chicken, fish, or horsemeat. According to the ancient records, it was believed that these foods caused sores on the skin. And so they might, in people who are allergic to them.

Ancient Egyptian tablets tell about the death of King Menes in 2641 B.C. The king was stung by a hornet, and the vivid details of his symptoms, inscribed in hieroglyphics, sound just like a modern case history.

Many of the laws in the Old Testament are careful rules about which foods may be eaten and which may not. There are even rules that forbid the mixing of certain types of foods with others. Many scholars believe that there were sound practical reasons behind these religious laws. Pork, one of the forbidden foods, may be infested with worm parasites, which can make people ill or even kill them. Shellfish may carry poisons, especially in the summer months. Some scholars suggest that observations of common food allergies may have prompted some of the dietary laws. Indeed, modern allergy specialists know that often certain combinations of foods will produce an allergic reaction even when the individual foods can be eaten alone without harm.

The Babylonian Talmud, a collection of history, laws, and legend compiled by Jewish rabbis and scholars in the fifth century A.D., goes farther. It contains a description of a practical method to help people who suffer from stomach pains or diarrhea after eating eggs. According to the Talmud, the person should eat a very small amount of egg each day and then, very slowly and gradually, increase the amount eaten. This is exactly the method allergists today use in trying to "desensitize" people who are allergic to eggs or other foods that are difficult to avoid or cannot be eliminated from the diet.

In the first century B.C., the Roman poet and philosopher Lucretius wrote, "One man's meat is another man's poison." This old, familiar saying is now used about anything that is good for some people and bad for others, but Lucretius probably meant it literally. What is good food for most people may truly be a poison for someone who is allergic to it.

Hippocrates, the Father of Medicine, who lived from about 460 to 377 B.C., described cases of *asthma*, which means "panting" in Greek. He also wrote, "It is a bad thing to give milk to persons having sick headaches." Scholars believe that the Greek physician may have been pointing out that an allergy to milk may be a cause of migraine headaches.

Another ancient physician, Aretaeus of Cappadocia, left a very detailed account of migraine, dated A.D. 110, describing the typical symptoms—an early phase of "lightning" flashes before the eyes, followed by headache and upset stomach. Aretaeus reported on cases of asthma, too. The second-century Greek physician Galen was quite familiar with migraine and also described people who always sneezed when they were in the presence of certain plants and flowers.

Through the centuries, reports from observant physicians continued to come in. Botallus, writing in 1565 about the duty of a doctor to his patient, mentioned Galen's observations and noted that he had seen similar cases. He said he'd known people "who, at the smell of roses, were seized with a loathing, as to be subject to headaches, or a sneezing fit, or a running of the nostrils, so that for two days it could not be stopped. ... I know, likewise, of a woman who, at the smell of must, would fall over, collapse ... be forced to vomit, or have a severe headache ... therefore doctors should refrain from using this perfume, or any other that may affect the patient."

Early in the nineteenth century, an English physician, John Bostock, contributed detailed descriptions of allergic reactions and speculated on their causes. Dr. Bostock had had plenty of opportunity to study allergy symptoms, for he himself had suffered from both hay fever and asthma since childhood. In an account published in 1828, Dr. Bostock used the term "hay fever" for the first time, to describe the sneezing, runny nose and eyes, itching throat, and generally miserable feeling that afflict some people during the summer. He used the name because in those days any sort of illness was referred to as a "fever," and this one occurred during the haying season. "Hay fever" is not really a very appropriate name, since fever is not one of the usual symptoms of the condition and hay does not cause it. But though medical specialists might prefer a more accurate name, such as "seasonal allergic rhinitis" (that is, an inflammation of the nose that results from an allergy in certain seasons of the year), the name "hay fever" stuck and is still used. Dr. Bostock was a careful observer of symptoms, but he was not very accurate at guessing their cause. He was convinced that hay fever was due to changes in temperature, and especially to the effects of heat and the summer sun.

In 1852, another hay fever sufferer, Dr. W. R.

A cold-water shower bath was a typical eighteenth-century treatment for hay fever. Like other treatments of the time, it didn't work very well.

Kirkman, discovered the real cause of hay fever by experimenting on himself. He was growing grasses in a hothouse, and a few days before Christmas—hardly the usual hay fever season—he collected some of the grass pollen, rubbed it on his hands, and sniffed it. Immediately he began to sneeze violently, and it was an hour later before he could stop. Dr. Kirkman published an account of his experience in a paper called "Case of Hay Fever," but the arguments in medical circles raged on. Years later, there were still physicians who claimed that hay fever was due to heat, sunshine, or vegetable matter in the air.

One of the great pioneers of allergy work, Dr. Charles Harrison Blackley of Manchester, England, finally resolved the controversy with a series of experiments in which he invented methods that allergists still use today. Dr. Blackley was also a hay fever sufferer and served as his own first guinea pig. His interest in studying allergy began when he accidentally bumped into a vase of grasses that his children had arranged, and promptly began to sneeze. Deciding that grass pollen must be causing his hay fever attacks, Dr. Blackley carefully collected pollen from flowers of Italian ryegrass. He scratched a small spot on one forearm with a lancet and applied the pollen to it. Then he scratched a similar spot on the other forearm but did not place any pollen on it. The spot that had received the pollen began at once to itch maddeningly, and the area around it swelled up in an enormous hive. The scratched spot on the other arm did not show any sign of swelling or irritation. Later, Dr. Blackley showed that only people who suffered from hay fever developed redness and swelling when grass pollen was applied on a scratch; people who were not allergic had no reaction. Today

Allergists still use skin tests. In this modern version, antigens are placed on the patient's arm, which is then pricked with the device shown.

PHOTO BY CHARLES HAYS

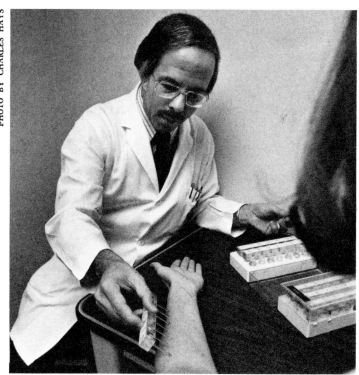

allergists use variations of Dr. Blackley's original scratch test not only for hay fever but also for allergies to numerous pollens, molds, dust, foods, and other substances.

Charles Blackley made many suggestions for further studies. He thought that pollen grains, tiny particles that transmit plants' reproductive cells, contain some sort of toxin, or poison. In the years that followed, medical scientists learned how to immunize people against diseases such as diphtheria by taking toxins from bacteria, changing them into a form called toxoids, and then injecting them. The person's body would then produce antitoxins, which would protect the person from getting the disease.

In 1911, a London physician, Charles Noon, suggested that people could be immunized against pollen toxin in the same way. But he did not know how to change the pollen to make it "nontoxic." So, instead, he developed a different method. He injected tiny amounts of pollen extracts—too small to cause any harm—and then, over a period of many weeks and months, gradually increased the dose. Eventually the patients became less sensitive and were able to tolerate the pollen blowing through the air during the pollen season without getting hay fever attacks. Some of Dr. Noon's ideas were incorrect—the pollen "toxin," for example, is not a true toxin, since for most people it is perfectly harmless—and he did not really understand how his method worked. But it did work, and it remains a method of long-term treatment that helps many allergy patients.

Another of Dr. Blackley's ideas that later proved very useful was that of studying the amount of pollen in the air. He put oiled microscope slides in various places—in the city and in the countryside—and then counted the number of pollen grains that stuck to the oily surface. He noticed that the higher the "pollen count," the more he and other hay fever victims sneezed. Today pollen counts are made in much the same way, and the results are announced on the radio and TV during the hay fever season.

Around the turn of the century, studies began to cast light on another important aspect of allergy. The technique of immunization saved the lives of many people who would have died of diseases. But some puzzling results were obtained. Sometimes a patient who received an injection of an antitoxin or serum to protect him from a disease would develop a whole set of symptoms quite different from those of the disease. Sometimes the reactions to the injection were even more severe than the disease it was meant to prevent. Typically, they occurred after the *second* injection of antitoxin or serum, not the first. The unfortunate patients were apparently developing a sensitivity to something else in the serum, even while they were being protected from the disease. Diphtheria and tetanus antitoxins, for example, are produced by injecting the toxoid into a horse, whose body can manufacture large amounts of the protective material. The antitoxin is then obtained from the horse's blood. But it contains typical horse proteins as well. So a person who develops a reaction after an immunization has become sensitized to the horse proteins. He is now allergic to the serum.

This whole sequence of events was not clearly understood back in 1900. But important progress was made with the experiments of a French researcher, Charles Richet. During the years between 1889 and 1902, Dr. Richet and his associates were cruising on the Indian Ocean with the prince of Monaco, studying the problem of the hives caused by contact with the stingers of the Portuguese man-of-war, a kind of jellyfish. After he returned to Paris, Dr. Richet studied another stinging creature, the sea anemone, looking for the toxin that produced the hives. He injected the toxin into dogs and nothing happened. But when the dogs received a second injection of the sea anemone toxin, serious symptoms resulted. Sometimes the dogs died. Dr. Richet and his co-workers repeated the experiments and noticed that at least a few days must pass between the first and second injection for the serious reaction to occur. They recognized that the reactions they had observed were similar to those of serum sickness that people sometimes get to antitoxins prepared in horses. Dr. Richet named the reaction *anaphylaxis*, meaning "without protection"— the opposite of *prophylaxis*, which means "protection." This discovery won Dr. Richet a Nobel Prize.

The term "allergy" was not used until 1906, when it was proposed by a Viennese pediatrician, Clemens von Pirquet, who believed that the term "anaphylaxis" was not general enough. "Allergy" means a changed or different reactivity. Allergic people do not react to certain substances the same way most people do. Dr. von Pirquet suggested that a substance that stimulates a change in reaction should be called an "allergen." He noted that the poison of mosquitoes and bees, the pollen that causes hay fever, and the hive-producing substances of strawberries and crabs could all be classed as allergens. One reviewer who commented on Dr. von Pirquet's scientific paper claimed that it was unimportant and merely introduced a new and useless term. Today no one remembers the name of the reviewer, and allergy—the area of study described by Dr. von Pirquet—is an important field of medical science.

What Is Allergy?

Ragweed plants ripening in an open field release tiny pollen grains, which are carried off by the summer breezes. A few miles away, some of these pollen grains are inhaled by a hay fever sufferer, and soon he begins to sneeze. Yet his wife, sitting right beside him and breathing the same pollen-laden air, has no reaction at all.

What happens in an allergy victim's body during an allergic reaction? Why do some people have allergies, while others don't? Gradually, especially in the last decade or two, pieces of the allergy puzzle have begun to fall into place. Scientists now know the answers to many of the questions of allergy and are following up promising leads toward new discoveries.

One thing that is now firmly known is that allergies are associated with the working of the body's immune system. Normally the body defenses protect us from harm. But in allergies, these defenses go out of control. In attempting to protect the body from substances that are not real threats, they themselves cause harm.

Life is a constant struggle. The body is continually being challenged by invading bacteria and viruses. Harmful or poisonous substances are being inhaled or swallowed and must be gotten rid of or changed somehow, so that they will not damage the body tissues. Even inside the body tissues, cells are continually wearing out and dying, and means must be provided to take them apart, recycle the useful materials, and get rid of whatever is left over. Sometimes cells become changed and begin to run wild; these renegade body cells must be promptly weeded out before they can grow into cancers that may overwhelm the body and kill.

One of the body's main lines of defense against foreign invaders and enemies within is a type of white blood cells called lymphocytes. These cells ceaselessly patrol the body, traveling through the bloodstream and squeezing in and out of the tissues. They act as a kind of combined force of watchmen, policemen, soldiers, and garbage collectors. There are two main types of lymphocytes, each with their own special jobs. One type, the T-lymphocytes (so named because they have spent some time in or been influenced by a structure called the thymus gland), specialize in recognizing which substances belong in the body and which do not. T-cells can send out chemical messages to summon white blood cells called macrophages to gobble up foreign invaders. The T-cells make some chemical weapons of their own, to attack cancer cells and other cells and substances that do not belong in a healthy body. And the T-cells can help the second type of lymphocytes, the B-cells (which come from the lymph nodes and other parts of the body). The main job of the B-lymphocytes is to produce substances called antibodies.

Invading bacteria, like all cells, are made up of chemicals, and the chemicals on their surface form characteristic patterns and shapes which are different for each kind of cell. Antibodies are chemicals, too. They are proteins, made up of thousands of tiny chemical building blocks called amino acids. For any large foreign chemical that enters the body—for instance, the coating on the outside of a bacterium—there are antibodies produced that can neatly fit together with it, like the fit of a key in a lock. Once antibodies have been matched up with the invading chemicals, called antigens, the body can keep copies of these antibodies on hand as patterns. If, later, there is a new invasion of the same kind of antigens, cells in the lymph nodes can mass-produce antibodies to cope with them—as many as are needed. That is a way we can gain immunity to some diseases—either by having the disease and recovering from it, or by receiving injec-

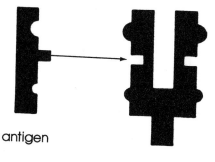

Antigens and antibodies fit together like a key in a lock.

antigen

antibody

tions of a vaccine containing antigens that will stimulate antibody production.

The antibodies form a class of body chemicals called immunoglobulins. Scientists have found five kinds of immunoglobulins in people's blood: immunoglobulins G, M, A, D, and E (or IgG, IgM, IgA, IgD, and IgE for short). IgG, the gamma globulins, make up nearly three-quarters of the globulins in blood serum. These are the globulins mainly responsible for defending the body against bacteria and viruses. For a long time, scientists believed that the globulins were involved in allergic reactions, but they were not sure which one was the "allergy globulin." In the early 1960s, it was thought that the antibody that produced allergic reactions was a type of IgA. At that time, IgE had not been discovered, since blood serum contains only 1/100,000th as much IgE as IgG. But then an allergy researcher, Dr. Mary Loveless, found an allergy patient who suffered from a very rare hereditary condition. His blood contained no IgA at all—and yet he suffered from allergies. In 1966, a husband-and-wife team of allergy researchers at the Children's Asthma Research Institute and Hospital in Denver, Dr. Kimishige Ishizaka and Dr. Teruko Ishizaka, discovered IgE in the blood of allergy patients and proved that it was the globulin responsible for allergic reactions. They studied the IgE, and gradually they and other researchers worked out what happens when an allergen enters the body.

Picture a pollen grain floating through the air. It is tiny—too small to see without a microscope. It is inhaled into a person's nose and settles onto the lining of the nasal passage. The watery secretions on the nasal membrane begin to work on the pollen grain, breaking it down and releasing the chemicals it contains. Normally these chemical particles would be harmlessly whisked away in the flow of the mucus that coats the lining of the nose. But in a hay fever victim, the nasal membrane has larger-than-usual amounts of IgE molecules of types that match the pollen antigens. An IgE molecule is shaped like a Y. The tail of the Y can attach to particular spots on the surface of special cells called mast cells. The arms of the Y can grab hold of antigen molecules. Actually, two Y-shaped IgE molecules next to each other share

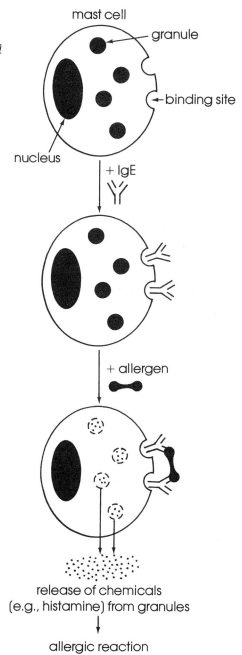

Y-shaped IgE molecules become attached to the mast cells. They combine with allergens and stimulate the mast cells to release histamine.

in holding the antigen, forming a bridge. When this IgE bridge is formed, tiny chemical packets inside the mast cells are stimulated to spill out their contents, which pass out of the mast cells. One of the main chemicals that the mast cells release is called histamine. It and other "allergy mediators" act on the cells around them, producing a number of effects. Histamine, for example, causes the blood capillaries to dilate (widen) and become sievelike, so that fluid from the blood can leak out into the tissues. Histamine can also cause smooth muscle— such as the muscle lining the breathing passages—to contract uncontrollably, and it stimulates the mucus-producing cells to work harder. If these reactions occur mainly in the nose, as in hay fever, the nasal membranes become swollen and watery. An allergic reaction in the eyes causes them to itch and produce tears. In the skin, allergic reactions cause the tissues to swell up into hives. An allergic reaction deep in the breathing passages, in the bronchi and bronchioles of the lungs, causes these air pipes to contract, while their linings swell, making it difficult to breathe. Allergic reactions in the stomach and intestines can produce painful cramps and diarrhea. Allergic reactions can also occur in the circulatory system, making the blood vessels "leaky."

The kind of allergic reaction that will occur when the body is challenged by an allergen depends on many things: the kind of allergen—pollen, mold, animal dander, a food chemical, insect venom, or a drug, for example; the way the allergen enters the body—by inhalation or swallowing; and where the greatest amounts of allergen-reactive IgE are concentrated. Some allergic people have the most allergen-reactive IgE in their nasal passages and suffer from hay fever. For others, the "shock organ" is the deeper breathing passages, and these people have asthma. (The same allergen may produce hay fever in one person and asthma in another.) In some allergic people, the most allergen-reactive IgE is found in the skin, and they suffer from hives and rashes. For someone whose skin is the allergic "shock organ," a skin reaction can result even though the allergen never touches the skin: people can get hives from foods they eat or from breathing animal dander.

Allergies are not contagious—you cannot "catch" hay fever or hives from someone else. But allergies do seem to be inherited, although they do not perfectly follow the simple rules of heredity that govern such traits as eye color and the shape of the nose. Allergists estimate that if one parent has allergies, about one-third of the children will develop allergies before they are ten years old. If both the father and the mother have allergies, about two-thirds of their children will probably have allergies of their own before the age of six. But the children will not necessarily have the same kinds of allergies as their parents. Only the tendency to have allergies is inherited. For example, in one family we know, the mother has suffered from hay fever since she was five, and the father breaks out in hives when he eats certain foods. One child has a slight sniffle and an itch at the back of his throat, which stay with him all year round and get a little worse in the summer. Another child had a terrible case of eczema on her face when she was an infant but does not seem to have any allergies now. Another child is so allergic to Brazil nuts that her whole face puffs up until her eyes are swollen shut if she eats a small piece of one; contact with guinea pigs produces the same alarming result, but she can play with rabbits, cats, dogs, and gerbils to her heart's content without the slightest reaction. And one child, now fifteen, has not shown any signs of allergies at all.

Some recent studies suggest that although a tendency for allergies is inherited, the first attack of actual allergic symptoms may be triggered by a respiratory infection caused by a virus. If these studies are confirmed, then the development of immunization against common respiratory disease viruses could prevent many children with allergic tendencies from becoming sensitized.

As with other antibodies, there are many kinds of immunoglobulins E, each able to react with a particular kind of antigen, or allergen. The reaction does not occur the first time the body meets the allergen, but only later, when the IgE-producing system has been stimulated. When this has occurred, copies of the appropriate IgE molecules are ready and waiting to spark an allergic reaction when the allergen appears again. A single exposure to the allergen can be enough to sensitize a person, or many contacts may be necessary. A person may suddenly become allergic to a pet dog, for example, after he or she has been living with the animal for years. Or one ragweed season too many may suddenly produce symptoms of hay fever. There are even people who develop allergies to some of their own body chemicals. Certain serious diseases, such as some types of arthritis and myasthenia gravis, are believed to be caused by reactions of this sort.

Fortunately, even the most allergic people do not become sensitized to *everything* in their environment. But it is common for people to have more than one allergy. People who have hay fever due to a ragweed pollen allergy, for example, are often aller-

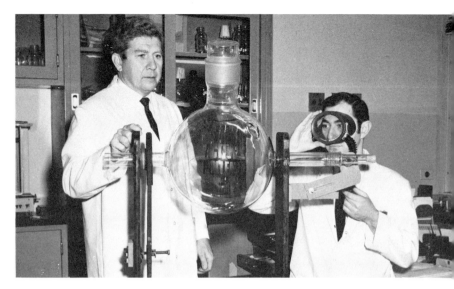

Allergy researcher Dr. John T. Connell is having a hay fever patient breathe a measured amount of ragweed pollen. Then the patient's nasal passages will be examined.

gic to dust and molds as well, and may have a few food allergies.

The amount of the allergen and the length of the exposure have a great influence on the severity of the symptoms that develop. An allergic person may not react at all to a small dose of an allergen, but may develop a severe reaction once the dose becomes large enough. Hay fever victims often find that their symptoms become much worse as the pollen season goes on. Allergists have observed that early in the season their patients may not react at all to a certain dose of pollen, but several weeks later a much smaller dose will spark a violent fit of sneezing. Apparently the nasal membranes become more sensitive as they are continually irritated by repeated attacks of the pollen grains and the levels of IgE antibodies in the body rise in response to the challenges of the allergen. Other allergies, too, may become worse when a person's IgE system is already stimulated. A hay fever victim may react badly to watermelon during the hay fever season, although he can eat it with less likelihood of trouble at any other time of the year.

It seems strange that the body should contain a substance like IgE, which can do it so much harm. But in many parts of the world, IgE may work as an important part of the body's defenses. Some scientists believe that this immunoglobulin is one of the body's means of protecting itself against worm parasites. Some studies have suggested that people with high IgE levels do not develop as severe symptoms when they are infected with such parasites.

The discovery of IgE and its role in allergy has brought new understanding of how allergic reactions occur, how the present tests and treatments for allergy work, and has pointed out ways that may lead to much better treatments in the future. But before we explore the exciting frontiers of allergy research, let's find out more about the various kinds of allergies and how they are diagnosed and treated.

Hay Fever

Many people who know a little bit about allergies believe that hay fever is commonly caused by flowers like roses or goldenrod. Indeed, the form of hay fever that occurs during the early summer is often called rose fever. But roses and other bright-colored, showy flowers are rarely to blame for the miseries of hay fever sufferers.

The most common cause of hay fever *is* flower pollen. Minute grains of pollen are formed in structures called anthers, which are usually borne on tiny stalks arranged around the center of a flower. The pollen grains contain reproductive cells that combine with other reproductive cells in another flower structure called the ovary. The fertilized egg cells that result from this combination develop into seeds, which can grow into a new generation of plants. But getting the pollen and the egg cells together can present some problems. Some plants have flowers that can fertilize themselves. But many must be cross-pollinated—pollen from the anthers of one flower must be carried to a flower on another plant for fertilization to occur and seeds to be formed.

Bright-colored flowers with large, showy petals are usually pollinated by insects. Perhaps a butterfly, alighting to sip some sweet nectar, brushes against the anthers and unintentionally picks up a load of pollen as well. When it visits another flower, some of the pollen it carries brushes off, and the reproductive cells the pollen contains can fertilize the second flower's egg cells. The pollen produced by insect-pollinated flowers—roses, for example—is typically rather sticky and too heavy to be windborne with ease. The tiny pollen grains may be studded with microscopic hooks or burrs that help them to cling to an insect's legs or body. Unless you actually buried your face in a bouquet of sweet-smelling roses, there would not be too much chance of rose pollen getting into your nose to irritate it.

Some plants, however, depend on the wind to pollinate their flowers. Many trees, grasses, and common weeds are wind-pollinated. Their flowers are not adapted to attract insects. Usually they are not sweet-smelling or bright-colored; indeed, wind-pollinated flowers are often so small and inconspicuous that you might not notice them at all. But they produce enormous amounts of a very light, fluffy pollen that is easily carried off by the slightest breeze.

The ragweed plant, for example, is Public Enemy No. 1 for millions of hay fever sufferers in

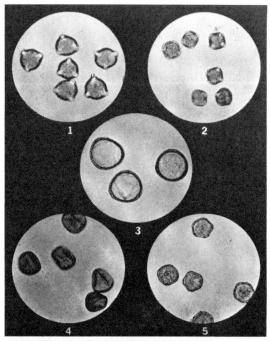

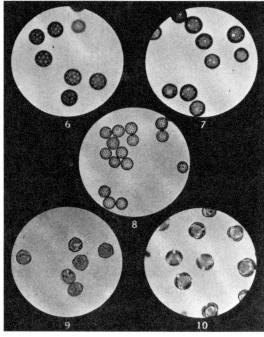

An assortment of pollen grains as seen under a microscope: (1) red oak; (2) ash; (3) hickory; (4) timothy; (5) elm; (6) Russian thistle; (7) English plantain; (8) short ragweed; (9) hemp; (10) sagebrush.

the United States. In much of the country, it begins to bloom around the middle of August and continues through September, until the first real frost kills off the plants. Ragweed flowers may not look like much, but they are incredible pollen factories. In one season, a single ragweed plant can produce as many as 8 *billion* pollen grains. These tiny, light, dry grains are carried far and wide by the winds and breezes. Ragweed pollen has been found as high as ten thousand feet (nearly two miles up), and as far as four hundred miles out to sea.

Because the pollen spreads so easily, it's hard to find anywhere to escape it entirely, but of course the pollen "pollution" of the air is densest in areas where there are many ragweed plants. Ragweed and other common hay fever provokers thrive in agricultural areas and on uncultivated land—open fields and vacant lots. In New York City, during the ragweed season, there is an average of 25 grains of ragweed pollen in each cubic yard of air, compared with averages of only 0.2 in San Francisco and a whopping 148 in Omaha. But sometimes the pollen counts can rise much higher. In New York City, counts as high as 1,000 ragweed pollen grains per cubic yard of air or more have been recorded.

Most hay fever sufferers in the United States are allergic mainly to ragweed pollen, and they are in misery in late summer, from mid-August to the end of September. The ripening of ragweed depends on the length of the days and nights, which changes with the changing seasons. In the southern United States ragweed ripens earlier, and since the weather is milder, the pollen season usually lasts farther into the fall. In the northern states the pollen season is later and shorter.

There are two other major hay fever seasons in the United States. One is in the early spring, sometime between February and April, depending on the locality. This is the time when the trees are bloom-

These are common culprits that cause hay fever misery: giant ragweed and short ragweed.

ing and tree pollen fills the air. The other major pollen season is in the late spring and early summer, from late April to early July, when the grasses are blooming. Many hay fever sufferers who are allergic to ragweed pollen also have grass allergies.

Pollen is not the only thing that can produce the sniffles, sneezes, and running eyes and nose of hay fever. Some hay fever sufferers are allergic to certain molds. Molds, such as the mildew that can ruin damp clothes and furnishings and the fluffy growth that forms on old bread and other bits of garbage, reproduce by sending enormous numbers of tiny reproductive particles called spores into the air. In most areas, except for the very warmest, outdoor molds tend to be seasonal allergens, occurring mainly from the spring to late fall. Unlike ragweed pollen, mold spores do not disappear with the first killing frost, since some molds can grow on dead vegetation. Snow lowers the mold count; then when the snow thaws, the molds can grow again. But they grow faster in warmer temperatures. A damp basement, a refrigerator drip pan, or the hay in a barn may provide "hot spots" where molds can grow—and send their spores into the air—all year round.

In addition to the seasonal hay fever sufferers, there are many who have hay fever–like symptoms throughout the year. Calling this condition hay fever

This is what one type of mold looks like under a microscope. Notice all the tiny spores ready to float out into the air.

seems like stretching things a bit too far, so doctors prefer to use the term "perennial allergic rhinitis." Some of the people who suffer from perennial allergic rhinitis also have one or more of the seasonal forms of hay fever, since it is common for allergy sufferers to be sensitive to more than one allergen.

Tracking down the cause of a particular case of perennial allergic rhinitis can often be a real job for a medical detective. For some people it turns out to be a sensitivity to the hair or dander of a pet. Allergies have been observed not only to cats and dogs, but to horses, small rodents such as mice, and birds (including chickens and parakeets). Often a person allergic to one kind of animal is also sensitive to other animals in the same family. Someone allergic to house cats, for example, may start coughing and sneezing after a visit to the lion house at the zoo. But some people are allergic to just one species of animal. If a pet to which a person is severely allergic dies or has to be given away, though, it is usually best not to take the chance of trying to replace it with another animal, since the new pet may turn out to be allergy-producing too. Sometimes an allergy to an animal may develop suddenly, after weeks, months, or even years of daily contact with no ill effects. Banishing the pet from the bedroom or keeping it outdoors most of the time may be enough to keep a mild pet allergy under control. If the allergy is severe, brief contact or just the residues of hair and dander in the house may spark a violent allergic reaction.

Some people are allergic to perfumes, hair sprays, or other products for personal or household use. Allergists sometimes hear tragic-comic tales about husbands or wives who become allergic to each other and cannot go near their spouses without suffering from a runny nose and sneezes. Often the problem turns out to be an allergy to the body powder that the wife uses, the husband's shaving lotion, or some other product. A change to a different brand restores the happy marriage. One of the most common year-round allergies is to household dust. You must have noticed that no matter how often you clean your house, a thin layer of fluffy, whitish dust keeps forming on the furniture, woodwork, lampshades, and just about everything else in the house. If you look at the path of a sunbeam shining in through the window, you can see tiny dust particles dancing in the air. House dust is made of bits of fluff that come from the breakdown of fabrics such as carpets, curtains, and upholstered furniture and from the stuffings of pillows and mattresses. Tiny scaly particles from the skin of people and animals also get into the air.

For a long time, allergists were puzzled by dust allergies. Often patients would show no sensitivity at all to the individual components of dust—fabrics, feathers, mattress padding, for example—yet were severely allergic to extracts of household dust. Something more seemed to be added when the individual bits got together to form dust. Recently, researchers have found that microscopic mites of a species called *Dermatophagoides pteronyssinus* thrive in household dust. Tests have shown that many of the patients who are allergic to house dust are actually allergic to these mites.

Dust allergies persist all year round, but they tend to be worst in the winter months. There are two main reasons for this: first, people stay inside more during the winter and tend to keep the windows and doors shut, so that all the dust stays in the house; and second, when the heat is kept on in the winter, the air is usually rather warm and dry, so that dust particles are easily carried through the air, and the nasal membranes become dry and more easily irritated. Symptoms of dust allergy also tend to get worse when the person is sleeping, because of particles from the bedding and mattress.

The nose is the gateway to the respiratory system, and it is the major "shock organ" in hay fever. In addition to the annoying drip and difficult breathing, people with untreated hay fever may also develop nasal polyps, grapelike growths inside the nose. The nasal passages have a number of connections with other tubes and cavities, and the allergic problems frequently spread. The sinuses, hollow cavities inside the bones of the forehead and cheeks, drain into the upper air passages of the nose. When the nasal membranes are swollen, they may close off the openings into the sinuses, trapping mucus inside

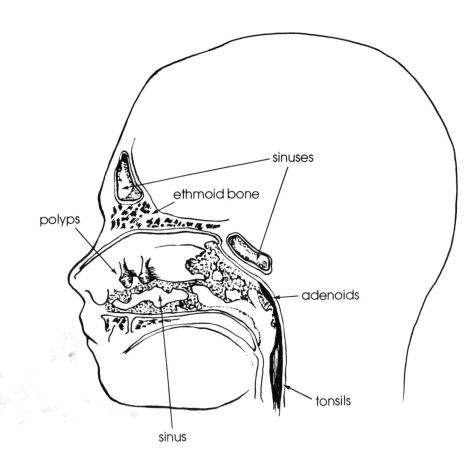

The inside story of the upper respiratory tract.

them and providing a fine breeding ground for bacteria. Sinus infections are a frequent complication of allergic rhinitis. The nasal passages also connect with the throat and with the eustachian tubes that lead to the ears. The allergic inflammation of the membranes can spread to these areas, producing a maddening itching sensation and opening the way to infection. Allergic children often suffer from earaches and a partial loss of hearing that comes and goes. All these symptoms can result in repeated loss of sleep, making the hay fever sufferer chronically tired and irritable.

The same allergens that cause hay fever and other forms of allergic rhinitis can also produce symptoms deeper in the respiratory tract, in the bronchi and bronchioles. Indeed, some hay fever patients also develop bronchial asthma.

Asthma

An asthma attack can be a terrifying experience for the sufferer. It's frightening, too, for someone who is watching a child or a friend gasping for breath. An attack starts with a feeling of tightness in the chest, which gets tighter and tighter, as though a giant hand were squeezing. It gets hard to breathe. The asthma patient opens his mouth and gasps, trying to get more air. Breathing out seems to take a special effort. Lying down just makes things worse, bringing a choking feeling. As the asthma patient battles for breath, neck and chest and stomach muscles knot and strain. Thick mucus gathers in the bronchial tubes, and the patient tries vainly to cough it up. Sweating, exhausted, and fighting for air, he wheezes noisily and may turn slightly blue. The attack can last for hours, or, if it is not treated, may go on for days or weeks.

Nine million Americans now suffer from asthma, and their numbers are growing. Asthma may strike young children and, if not effectively treated, may limit and handicap their lives. Some children's attacks gradually grow less severe. But asthma also strikes many adults, who may develop the condition in middle or old age, and their attacks may get worse as the years go by. Like hay fever, asthma may be seasonal, caused by allergies to pollen or mold spores. In other cases, asthma attacks may occur at any time of year, or even so often that they are almost continuous. If asthma is not treated and controlled, the attacks tend to get more frequent and more serious.

Normally the breathing passages have a very effective system for getting rid of bits of dust, smoke particles, and other foreign materials that are inhaled. The linings of all the branching tubes are coated with a watery, slightly slimy mucus. Cells lining the breathing passages are studded with microscopic cilia, tiny hairlike structures which wave back and forth continually, setting up currents in the mucus that flow toward the mouth. These currents sweep the tiny foreign particles up into the throat, where they are usually swallowed and eliminated through the digestive tract.

But in people who have asthma, histamine and other chemicals involved in allergic reactions cause the membranes lining the bronchial tubes to swell. The muscles of the tubes contract, making the airways smaller. Meanwhile, the mucus-secreting cells work overtime, producing thick mucus plugs. Breathing becomes more and more difficult. Air is trapped in the tiny air sacs of the lungs and may stretch and

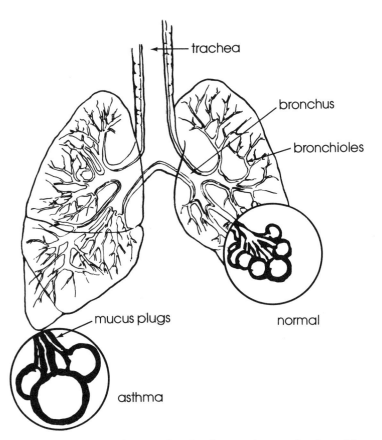

Asthma causes changes in the lungs that make breathing difficult.

damage them. During an asthma attack, some of the tiny cilia on the lining cells are destroyed. The patient is thus more likely to get another attack, since the system for expelling bacteria, allergens, and pollution particles does not work as well as it used to. The flow of mucus is slower, too, and in the stagnant

54

pools deep in the lungs, bacteria can thrive. Asthma patients are very susceptible to bronchial infections. And infections can trigger new asthma attacks.

Most cases of asthma are caused by allergens that are inhaled, such as pollen, molds, dust, and animal dander. But allergies to food can also cause asthma. So can drug allergies. Many asthma attacks are provoked by a sensitivity to aspirin. (This is an important fact for doctors to remember, for aspirin is a commonly used remedy for some of the symptoms of asthma.)

Air pollution is playing a growing role in causing asthma. When smog blankets a city, asthma patients flock to the doctors and hospitals for treatment, and very severe smogs cause many asthma deaths. Experiments have shown that common ingredients of polluted air, such as ozone, sulfur dioxide, nitrogen dioxide, and cigarette smoke, damage lung tissue, causing histamine to be released.

For a while it was fashionable for doctors to believe that asthma is mainly a psychological disease, caused by emotional problems rather than physical factors. When a child with asthma was brought in for treatment, some doctors would probe into the home background, often making the parents and child even more nervous and upset than they already were. But what about patients who suffered from asthma only in August and September and gave positive tests for allergy to ragweed pollen? Or children who tested allergic to animal dander and whose asthma disappeared when a pet dog or cat was given away? It did not seem very sensible to think that such cases of asthma were due to an insecure home life or other problems. Emotions may trigger or aggravate a particular asthma attack, but only in a person who is already an asthma sufferer and thus has easily irritated bronchial air passages.

Today most doctors believe that emotional problems play an important role in asthma, but mainly as effects, not causes. An asthma patient lives with fear —fear of suffocating while an attack is in process and fear of the next attack when breathing is normal. Anything—a food, some substance in the air, physical exertion, excitement (even happy excitement)— may trigger a sudden gasping for breath. Having to limit activities and losing time from school or work may make the asthma patient feel "different." He or she may become irritable or depressed. Friends and relatives may overreact, treating the asthma patient with pity or fear and increasing the emotional difficulties.

Effective treatment of asthma is important to avoid these problems, to help an asthmatic child develop as normally as possible—both physically and emotionally—and to keep an asthmatic adult from developing more serious disabilities. If asthma continues untreated, complications may occur. The secondary infections that the asthma patient develops so readily, and irritation from smoking or air pollution, may lead to chronic bronchitis (an inflammation of the bronchial tubes). Continual forced breathing may result in changes similar to emphysema, a condition in which the tiny air sacs in the lungs become damaged and stretched out, so that they cannot deliver enough oxygen to the blood. A person with emphysema becomes short of breath after the slightest exertion, and the continual strain of labored breathing and the poor oxygen supply can eventually damage the heart as well. Unlike the emphysema that older people may develop from other causes, the "pre-emphysema" to which untreated asthma may lead in children can be reversed by proper medical treatment, and the lung tissue can be restored to normal.

There are two parts to the treatment of asthma: immediate measures to cope with the medical emergency of an acute asthma attack, and long-term treatments to prevent further attacks.

When an attack is coming on, immediately taking a bronchodilator drug, which widens the bronchial tubes, can help to keep the attack mild and

brief. Bronchodilators can be taken in pill form or inhaled in the form of sprays. (But some studies indicate that improper use or overuse of aerosol sprays by asthma patients can sometimes make their asthma worse rather than better.) Drinking a lot of liquids is important, to keep the mucus thin and watery and easy to bring up. Drugs containing chemicals similar to caffeine (the stimulant in coffee or tea) can help since they dilate the bronchial tubes. Inhaling steam or cool mist can help to ease breathing and loosen and thin the mucus. Sedatives that relax the muscles can also be helpful, but they are tricky and should be used only with extreme caution and only when necessary, since they depress the

Breathing exercises can help asthma patients.

breathing too much. If an attack is very severe, a doctor may have to give the patient an injection of a strong bronchodilator such as Adrenalin, and perhaps oxygen to breathe.

Some of the newer asthma drugs, such as cromolyn sodium, act on the histamine release mechanism and can help to prevent asthma attacks. General exercises to build up the asthmatic's strength and resistance, and special breathing exercises, seem to be helpful in many cases. But as in other allergic conditions, the best long-term treatment is to discover what is causing the asthma and then find ways to protect the patient against it, either by avoiding the allergen or by attempting to lessen sensitivity with injection treatments in cases where this can be done.

Food Allergies

What's wrong with that baby? He's always spitting up some of his milk, and sometimes he vomits up a whole feeding. Between feedings, he cries with colic pains. He isn't gaining weight the way he should. And it's getting worse. For the past few days he has had diarrhea almost constantly. The food goes through him so fast that he isn't getting much nourishment and he's losing fluids faster than he can drink. He might die! Then the doctor changes his formula to a soybean milk substitute, and it's like a miracle. The new food stays down, and the colic and diarrhea stop. The baby begins to gain weight and thrive. His problem was a simple one and not too rare: he is allergic to cow's milk.

For most people, milk is a safe and nourishing food. But for some it is like a poison. Milk is one of the common foods to which people may be allergic. Other frequent troublemakers are eggs, wheat, corn, fish, shellfish, berries, nuts, chocolate, peas, beans, tomatoes, and oranges. There are *some* people who are allergic to nearly every food that people have ever eaten. Today, when more than three thousand food additives are used in prepared foods, the problem is even more complicated. Some people are allergic to the natural or artificial colorings, flavorings, thickeners, preservatives, and other additives.

Food allergies can cause a variety of symptoms. The foods come in contact with the lining of the digestive tract, and the allergens may act directly, producing local reactions such as sores in the mouth, spasms of the stomach or intestines (a baby's "colic" pains, for example), or diarrhea. As foods are digested, the chemicals they contain are absorbed into the bloodstream. Food allergens can cause reactions

Some of the common food allergens.

anywhere in the body, depending where a person's characteristic "shock organ" may be.

Skin reactions such as urticaria (hives) and eczema are frequent reactions to food allergies. Allergies to particular foods can cause headaches. Allergists find that hay fever or asthma patients who have not been helped by the usual injections for ragweed pollen, dust, or other common inhaled allergens can often be more effectively treated by identifying and eliminating food allergies.

A controversial area of modern allergy research is the possible link of food allergies to behavior problems in children. Some physicians have suggested that allergic reactions might make children tense and anxious and lead to behavior changes. These physicians believe that, in susceptible people, allergens can act directly on the nervous system.

Reactions to food allergies depend on many things, especially on the amount of the food consumed, the way it is taken, and how allergic the person is. Someone with a mild allergy may be able to eat small amounts of the food without trouble. Another person may be so sensitive to shrimp, for example, that he goes into a near-fatal anaphylactic shock after eating a dish of egg foo young that was cooked in a pan previously used for shrimp. President Jimmy Carter's brother Billy, who manages the family's peanut business, is allergic to peanuts. He can handle them with no ill effects (probably because the allergen is not absorbed in such contact), but if he eats just one peanut his face swells and his throat closes. Some people, however, are so sensitive to certain food allergens that even smelling them can bring a reaction. Cooking changes some of the chemicals foods contain, especially the proteins. (And proteins are common allergy-producers.) So a person may be allergic to raw carrots, for example, but not to cooked carrots.

In general, an allergic reaction to a food, as to other allergens, will not occur the first time the food is eaten, but rather the second time or later. Yet sometimes a baby shows a milk allergy right after it is born. And allergy tests of children sometimes show sensitivity to foods the child has never eaten. How can this be? Doctors think that in such cases the baby may have become sensitized to foods eaten by the mother before the child was born or while she was nursing it, if she breastfed.

Foods may also carry hidden ingredients. A person may think she is allergic to milk, when actually she is reacting to traces of an antibiotic that was used to treat the cow that gave the milk. During the Second World War, some English babies developed eczema when they drank an English brand of evaporated milk, but their skin problems cleared up when they were given American evaporated milk. It turned out that the English cows had been fed a fishmeal supplement, and the children were allergic to the fish proteins.

An allergy to one food is often accompanied by a sensitivity to other foods closely related to it. A person allergic to apples may also be allergic to pears; a wheat allergy may be coupled with allergies to other grains like rye; allergies to chicken and turkey may go together. Some other commonly eaten food families that may produce cross-sensitivities in allergic persons are: citrus fruits—oranges, grapefruits, lemons, and limes; stone fruits—peaches, apricots, cherries, and almonds; cucurbits—watermelons, cucumbers, squash; legumes—peas, beans, peanuts; mustard and cabbage; all fish; and shellfish such as crabs, lobsters, and shrimp. Such cross-sensitivities occur because closely related plants or animals share many chemicals in common. But some people are allergic to only one food in a particular group, since each kind of food has some chemicals that are found only in it.

Food allergies are often worse during a pollen season, when the person's IgE system is already stimulated. Some food allergies many appear to be seasonal when they are not, because many foods are most plentiful in certain seasons. An occasional peach dessert, eaten during the winter or spring, may produce no symptoms; but then during the summer, when fresh peaches are plentiful, the person may eat several peaches at a time and break out in hives or sneezes. (Since allergens may be changed chemically by cooking or baking, the difference in reaction may also depend on whether the fruits are eaten cooked or raw.)

An allergy patient is often asked to keep a food diary, writing down everything that is eaten for a week or two. A food diary can provide important clues to possible food allergies, but there are many things that can confuse the work of the doctor-detective. First of all, there are two types of allergic reactions to food: immediate and delayed. A person may react within minutes after eating a particular food—or even while the food is still being chewed. Or an hour or two may pass before the symptoms appear. Doctors believe that the immediate allergic reactions are sparked by allergens contained in the foods themselves, which act directly on the sensitive cells of the body. The delayed reactions may be caused by a sensitivity to chemicals that are formed when the foods are digested. It is often very hard to relate a delayed reaction correctly to the food that caused it, since other things may have been eaten in the meantime.

Another problem is that often it is almost impossible to tell exactly what you have eaten. Today we eat many processed foods, which may contain literally dozens of natural and artificial ingredients. Government regulations require that ingredients must be listed on labels. But in many cases, not *all* the ingredients need be listed, and those that are may be described in vague terms, such as "vegetable protein." Vague labeling can cause a lot of needless misery for people with food allergies. In addition, unsuspected food substances may be found in other products we deal with. A person allergic to cottonseed oil, for instance, may not realize that not only is it found in margarines, salad oils, and mayonnaises, but that many cakes, breads, canned and frozen fish, popcorn, potato chips, and candies are made with it; that it may be present in milk if the cows were fed cottonseed; and that this oil is used in cosmetics, fertilizer, animal feed, and in the production of paper, salt, machine tools, paint, and varnish. (The actual allergen in a cottonseed oil allergy is not the oil itself, but cottonseed proteins that are not completely removed when the oil is processed.) Soybeans, rich in high-quality protein, are being used more and more widely as a meat extender and flour enricher, and a list of the industrial products in which they are used would fill up this page.

Another difficulty in diagnosing food allergies is that food allergies may change, especially in young children. A sensitivity to a particular food may suddenly appear, and after a time, just as mysteriously, the child no longer seems sensitive and can eat the food with no ill effects.

Some doctors believe that people have a sort of instinctive aversion to the foods that may give them difficulty, so a listing of a patient's particular food dislikes should provide a good starting point in looking for possible food allergens. (You might wonder why allergies to foods a person dislikes would cause any problems, since he or she would tend to avoid them anyway. But sometimes people force themselves to eat foods they dislike—milk or eggs, for example—because they believe that the foods are particularly nourishing. And children often are given very little choice about which foods they may or may not eat.) This general rule frequently works out fairly well, but there are exceptions. Sometimes a person turns out to be allergic to some of his or her favorite foods. Chocolate is one of the common allergy provokers, yet most people love it.

It has even been suggested that a liking for a food a person is allergic to—and hence a frequent intake—may result in a certain tolerance to the food. One allergist tells of a young patient who was found to be terribly allergic to cow's milk. The allergist was interested in studying the heredity of allergies and asked the girl's father to try eliminating milk from his diet, too. The father had been suffering from some minor symptoms of chronic bronchitis all his life, and these went away when he stopped drinking milk, which he loved. But after a few weeks without milk, he happened to eat a small dish of cottage cheese and immediately had a severe attack of bronchitis. He had lost his tolerance for milk, and now even a small amount of a milk product resulted in more serious symptoms than he had had when drinking more than a quart of milk a day.

Skin Allergies

Do you know anyone who *doesn't* get a rash after contact with poison ivy? There are some people who are not sensitive to this irritating plant. The poison ivy rash is a true allergic reaction: it does not happen to everyone, and it never occurs after just one exposure. An allergic sensitivity must be developed.

The skin is a common "shock organ" for many allergens. Skin rashes and irritations may result from foods a persons eats or from drugs that are swallowed or injected. Less often they can result from allergens that are inhaled. But the most common type of allergic skin irritation is contact dermatitis, a reaction to something that actually touches the skin.

People vary in their sensitivity to skin irritants. Women's skin is usually more sensitive than men's. Fair skin is more susceptible to irritation than dark skin. Sweating makes the skin more sensitive, because chemicals in contact with the skin become moistened and may be more irritating. Physical health and the presence of other allergies can influence the sensitivity of the skin. Even the emotions can play a role—in some susceptible people symptoms are triggered by an exciting experience or an emotional upset.

Skin allergies may take the form of hives, single ones or clusters of them. These itchy swollen areas may go away without a trace in a few minutes or hours, or they may last for days. Skin allergies may appear as a fine rash or a patch of redness. The eyelids, tongue, hands or feet, or the entire body may swell. Allergies may cause tiny blood vessels in the

Urticaria, or hives, is a common skin reaction.

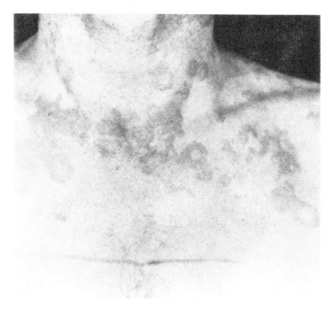

skin to leak, producing reddish-purple bruiselike marks called purpura. An itchy rash called eczema is very common in infants, often occurring on the cheeks, scalp, wrists, the bends of the elbows, and the creases behind the knees. Children, teenagers, and adults may also develop eczema, sometimes covering large parts of the body. The rash is so itchy that the person feels compelled to rub and scratch it; the skin often thickens and "weeps" with moisture that seeps out.

Eczema often affects infants.

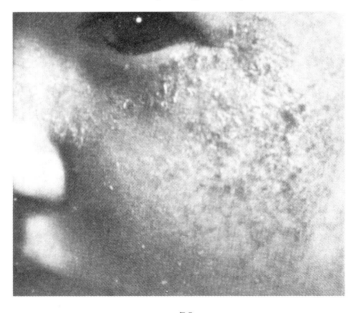

Hives and eczema, like hay fever, asthma, and food allergies, are IgE-type allergic reactions. Allergens taken into the body in various ways pass into the bloodstream and are carried to the skin tissues. In this "shock organ," sensitized IgE molecules, attached to mast cells, react with the allergens and trigger the release of histamines and other chemicals involved in the allergic response. Poison ivy rash and contact dermatitis, on the other hand, are allergic reactions of a different type, which scientists call cell-mediated immunity (CMI). This type of immunity involves T-lymphocytes. You may recall that one of the important jobs of the T-lymphocytes, white blood cells that patrol the tissues of the body, is to distinguish between the body's own chemicals and cells and foreign invaders such as bacteria. The T-cells can even tell the difference between normal body cells and cells that have changed and become cancerous. Once the enemies have been identified, the T-cells attack them and summon other defenders of the body to aid in the fight.

When poison ivy oil or some other allergenic chemical is in contact with the skin, roving T-lymphocytes detect the foreign chemicals and become sensitized. The sensitized T-cells multiply, and if the allergen is ever met again, they are ready to turn their powerful chemical weapons on it. Painful swell-

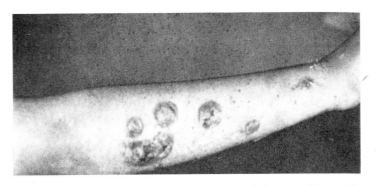

This case of contact dermatitis was caused by touching poison ivy.

ing and inflammation are side effects of the battle that results. Cell-mediated immunity is an important body defense that helps to protect us from infections and cancer. But the delayed hypersensitivity that results when T-lymphocytes use their weapons against an allergen is an annoyance rather than a help to the body.

A skin allergy that is caused by something eaten or injected or inhaled can pop out on almost any part of the body. But in contact dermatitis, the rash usually develops in the place actually touched by the allergen. The skin becomes red and itchy; it may swell or develop bumps or blisters. The location of the rash in contact dermatitis often provides a clue to what caused it. Swollen eyelids might indicate an allergy to eye makeup—or a habit of rubbing one's eyes after touching an allergen. Narrow, itchy red bands around a woman's waist and thighs would probably mean that she is allergic to the rubber in the elastic in her underwear. Allergies to metals might produce a rash on the wrist (from a wrist-watch or bracelet), neck (from a necklace), earlobes (from earrings), or fingertips (from handling coins). In one curious case, a woman suffered from blistered lips. The allergist tested her lipstick and various foods, but she was not allergic to any of them. Then a routine test showed that she was allergic to nickel. The allergist did not think this discovery solved the problem—until the woman came into his office one windy day and he saw her fixing her hair, holding her nickel-plated hairpins in her mouth as she did.

Cosmetics are frequently allergic offenders. Fabrics, furs, leathers, dyes, soaps, metals, rubber, and plastics can also cause contact dermatitis in susceptible people. When the major brands of laundry detergents added "enzyme" ingredients to the powders, allergists soon noted an increase in cases of contact dermatitis. People developed allergies to the new chemicals in the detergent residues that remain in clothes after washing. But the allergen to blame for a case of contact dermatitis need not be something new. Sometimes people suddenly become sensitive to something they have been exposed to for years.

Some people develop a curious allergy to the bacteria-killing ingredients that are added to certain brands of bath soap. The chemicals make their skin photosensitive—that is, they develop an allergic skin reaction if they go out into the sun after using the soap. (Photosensitivity can also be caused by perfumes and certain medications that are swallowed.)

Poison ivy is the most common of the irritating plants that can cause skin allergies. A person can get poison ivy by touching the plants (even by brushing against the twigs in the winter), by touching clothes that have become contaminated with the oil, or even by petting a dog that has run through poison ivy. Burning poison ivy plants is especially dangerous, for then the irritating chemicals go up in the smoke fumes and can be inhaled, causing a serious reaction in the lining of the bronchial tubes. The airborne droplets from burning plants can also cause contact dermatitis on the face, hands, and any other exposed areas of skin.

Poison ivy has always been a problem in America. The Indians warned the early settlers about it and its relatives, poison oak and poison sumac. About 70

75

Allergic people beware: (1) poison ivy; (2) poison oak; (3) poison sumac.

percent of all people can develop sensitivity to these plants, all of which contain an allergen called urushiol. Other plants, such as buttercups, poinsettias, daisies, tulips, philodendron, and tumbleweed can cause skin allergies in smaller numbers of people.

Insect Stings and Bites

It seems strange that a little thing like a bee can kill a human being. Actually the bee's venom is not that toxic. To kill, the bee needs help—from the victim's own body. The forty or so people who die each year from the stings of bees, wasps, and other insects die of anaphylactic shock, a severe allergic reaction of a body that has been sensitized to the insect venom by earlier stings.

There are more than one hundred thousand species of stinging insects, including about twenty thousand different species of bees alone. Some people who have suffered from severe reactions to stings have been found to be sensitive to the venom of more than one type of insect. Others are sensitive to just one kind of venom. The insects most likely to sting and cause serious reactions are the social insects, those which live together in large communities in hives or nests. These include many species of bees, wasps, hornets, and some ants.

A honeybee's stinger is barbed. It sticks in the skin of the victim and pumps venom into the skin as the bee struggles to get free; finally it rips off and

the injured bee dies, but her death is not much con-
solation for her victim. Wasps and hornets come
swarming out angrily if they believe that their nest is
being threatened. Their stingers are not barbed, so
they can sting again and again without harming themselves. The type of wasp called the yellow jacket
is especially aggressive. Yellow jackets are particularly short-tempered when they have been feeding
on fermented fruits in an orchard. (Like people,
wasps can get drunk!) They cause double trouble by

*Some poisonous insects can cause dangerous allergic reac-
tions.*

biting before they sting. The fire ants that are spreading through the southern United States are noted for the painful burning their stings cause; they can provoke serious allergic reactions. Less serious (non-anaphylactic) reactions have also been observed to the bites of mosquitoes, blood-sucking flies, fleas, and other biting insects.

When a bee or wasp stings, there is a pinprick sensation of pain. Normally a painful red swollen area then appears around the sting and gradually becomes surrounded by a white ring. The swelling usually goes down within a few hours, but itching, irritation, and a feeling of heat may persist for a day or two. Washing the area of the sting promptly with soap and water is helpful. (If a bee's stinger is still embedded in the skin, it should be scraped off with a fingernail as soon as possible, since it will continue to pump venom into the skin for a while even after it has broken off. Don't crush the bee or its stinger while it is still embedded, since you will be forcing more venom into the skin.) Ice cubes or ice packs applied directly to the area help to keep the venom from spreading. Vigorous exercise should be avoided, and the injured body part should be raised to decrease the circulation. Meat tenderizer solution, promptly applied to the sting, can help to destroy the venom. Antihistamine pills can cut down the itching, and

Close-up view of a bee's stinger left in the skin.

pain-killing ointments applied to the sting may also bring relief. The area of the body that was stung may determine how severe the reaction will be: a sting on an arm or leg is often less serious than one on the face or neck. If the stinger happens to puncture an artery or vein, a rapid and severe reaction may result.

Some beekeepers report that frequent stings have given them an immunity to bee venom, much like the lowered sensitivity that results from injections for pollen, mold, or dust allergies. But in some people, repeated stings have the opposite effect: they sensitize the person so that another sting can trigger a severe anaphylactic reaction.

Danger signals when a person has been stung by an insect are symptoms that occur somewhere else in the body or through the whole body, especially: large hives all over the body, a feeling of tightness in the throat or chest, a dry cough, sneezing, wheezing, a rapid pulse, a fall in the blood pressure, unusual redness or paleness of the skin, a sensation of heat all over the body, and a feeling of uneasiness and fear. These symptoms may quickly develop into dizziness, nausea, vomiting, cramps, difficulty in swallowing or breathing, and then unconsciousness. Anyone who experiences any of these symptoms after an insect sting (usually the early symptoms develop within two or three minutes) should go to a doctor or a hospital *right away*. Victims who die from an insect sting usually die within the first twenty minutes!

The emergency treatment for anaphylactic shock, whether caused by an insect sting, a drug, or a food to which the person is extremely sensitive, is a prompt injection of a drug called Adrenalin (or epinephrine). Epinephrine is actually a natural body chemical, produced by the adrenal glands in response to stress. Among other things, it dilates the bronchial tubes—making breathing easier—speeds up the heart, and channels much of the blood circulation away from the surface of the body and to the heart, lungs, and other important organs. The victim may have to be given oxygen, as well as antihistamines and other drugs.

When someone has had even a mild systemic (whole-body) reaction to an insect sting, the doctor may advise that he or she wear a medical identification tag with information on the insect sensitivity and carry an emergency kit containing antihistamines and a syringe filled with a premeasured dose of Adrenalin. If the person lives or works under conditions where further stings are likely, a series of injection treatments may be advisable. Tiny, carefully measured doses of extracts prepared from crushed insect bodies or doses of pure venom are injected into the skin about once a week, and gradually a tolerance is built up. (The pure venom provides more reliable protection and ways are being sought to make it more widely available.)

Everyone who may be sensitive to insect venom should follow commonsense precautions to avoid insect stings. Stay clear of hanging wasps' nests and piles of fallen leaves and dead logs that may hide a wasps' nest. Spray picnic areas with an insect repellant and keep garbage cans tightly closed. (Food attracts

A wasps' nest.

bees and wasps.) If you must walk through an area where insects are commonly found, wear light-colored, long-sleeved clothing and long pants. Avoid dark or bright colors, which seem to annoy bees and wasps, and leather clothing or other materials that have a rough texture or natural odor. Don't use perfumes and hair sprays with flower odors that bees and wasps might mistake for food. And if a bee or wasp flies around you or lands on your skin or clothing, don't thrash at it. (Stinging insects are more likely to attack rapidly moving objects.) Instead, stand still or continue walking slowly.

Drug Allergies

Penicillin, the first of the antibiotics, brought a dramatic revolution in the treatment of bacterial diseases. Millions of lives have been saved by this wonder drug and those that were developed after it. Yet sometimes, instead of curing, penicillin and other drugs can kill. It is estimated that at least one hundred Americans die each year from severe allergic reactions to penicillin. And 5 to 10 percent of the population will develop sensitivity to this drug at some time during their lives. The reactions may be quite varied, and not all are truly "allergic."

Some allergic reactions to penicillin are rather mild and typically occur after a time lag. As much as ten days after taking the drug, the patient may develop a rash or peeling skin over the whole body. A "serum sickness" reaction may occur—including hives, swelling, pain in the joints, and fever—usually lasting about two to three weeks. The kidneys and circulatory system may be affected.

If a mild reaction to penicillin is ignored and the drug is used again, a far more serious anaphylactic reaction may result in a small number of patients.

Doctors commonly keep a syringe of Adrenalin handy when they are giving a shot of penicillin. When the drug enters the bloodstream of a highly sensitized patient, he or she may have a serious reaction—perhaps even keel over suddenly and die within minutes. An immediate injection of Adrenalin and perhaps a tracheotomy to put an air tube down into the windpipe may be needed to save the patient's life; antihistamines, steroids, or other drugs commonly used to treat allergies simply do not work fast enough.

Penicillin seems to be one of the most readily sensitizing antibiotics. Indeed, doctors generally do not use penicillin ointments on the skin anymore because they so often cause contact dermatitis. But people can also develop allergies to other antibiotics. Many people have become sensitized to antibiotics because they are used so widely. Doctors may prescribe them even for colds and flu. Although these diseases are caused by viruses, against which antibiotics are ineffective, the drugs can prevent secondary bacterial infections. Antibiotics are also used to treat animals and may even be added routinely to animal feeds, on the theory that a chicken or steer, for example, that is healthy and free of bacterial infections will grow faster and be ready for the market sooner. Foods containing antibiotic residues are not supposed to be sold, but sometimes they slip through and may add to the possibility of sensitization.

Another common drug that can cause allergic reactions is aspirin. Most people can take this drug with no great harm, and use it for headaches, muscle aches, cramps, the feverishness of a cold, and numerous other minor ills. But when a person becomes sensitized to aspirin, a dose of this drug can cause reactions ranging from hives to asthma to a massive anaphylactic shock. Aspirin belongs to a class of chemical compounds called salicylates. Some people are allergic to aspirin alone, but others are allergic to salicylates in general. These people must learn to avoid not only aspirin (by itself and hidden in other common drug preparations such as Alka-Seltzer, Anacin, and numerous cold remedies) but also foods and flavorings that contain salicylates, for example, wintergreen flavoring, almonds, apples, cherries, grapes, oranges, peaches, raisins, strawberries, and wines.

Some people who take barbiturates (common ingredients of sleeping pills and sedatives) develop allergic reactions, including skin rashes, hives, and fever. This type of drug occasionally causes a curious kind of reaction in which a rash breaks out in one particular spot on the body—perhaps on one wrist or on the face —every time the drug is taken. People have also been reported to be sensitive to ointments and antiseptics containing mercury, drugs containing iodine, and the phenolphthalein ingredient in laxatives.

Sometimes it is difficult to determine whether a person is really sensitive to a drug or not. Many infectious diseases are accompanied by a skin rash, which may be mistaken for a drug reaction. Sometimes the person turns out to be sensitive not to the drug itself but to some additive in the drug—perhaps a coloring or flavoring. Changing to a different brand may permit the patient to tolerate the drug quite well.

Tests for sensitivity to penicillin and other drugs are being developed, but they are not yet available for wide use. It is best to report to your doctor any suspicions of drug sensitivity that have ever arisen and, in general, to avoid taking drugs to which you have had reactions in the past. Sometimes, however, a doctor must consider prescribing a drug despite a history of sensitivity if it is the best (or only) drug for treating a particular serious infection. For example, in bacterial endocarditis, a dangerous infection of the lining of the heart, penicillin can literally be lifesaving. The doctor may choose to give penicillin and be prepared to treat any complications that arise.

Immunizations can also cause allergic reactions.

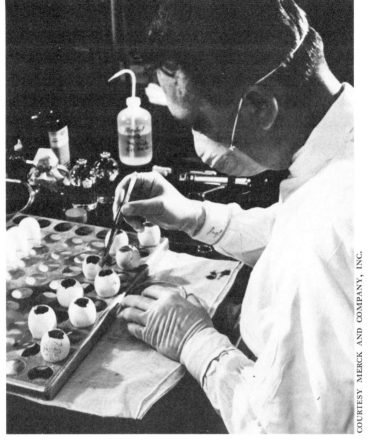

COURTESY MERCK AND COMPANY, INC.

Flu vaccine is prepared in chicken eggs. Egg allergens can cause allergic reactions to flu shots.

Antiserums prepared from horse serum are now much purer than they used to be, but if a person is extremely sensitive to horse proteins a reaction may still occur. People who are allergic to eggs may react badly to flu vaccine, since the viruses are grown on chick embryos. Gamma globulin, which is sometimes used to prevent viral diseases such as measles or hepatitis after a person has been exposed to a possible source of infection, has also been reported to trigger anaphylactic shock in some patients.

Allergic Headaches

Headaches are one of the most common ills that afflict us. Few people have never had a headache, and headaches are usually considered minor problems, but a persistent headache can make a person utterly miserable, affect behavior, and interfere with eating and sleeping to the point of undermining health.

Headaches are a symptom, not a disease, and they can have many causes, from simple muscle fatigue or eyestrain to hormone imbalances and brain tumors. Allergies are a major factor in many headaches. Painful sinus headaches can result when swollen nasal membranes block the drainage of the sinuses. Allergic reactions may affect the arteries leading to the brain, and the alternate stretching and relaxing of these blood vessels produces the familiar throbbing pain. Allergens may also cause an actual swelling of the brain tissues. Some reported causes of allergic headaches include inhalants such as animal dander, dust, pollen, and mold spores; foods such as milk, wheat, and chocolate; and drugs such as aspirin and phenolphthalein.

An allergic headache may occur immediately

after exposure to the allergen or with a delay of a few hours. Frontal headaches are one very common type of allergic headache. The pain is felt in the front of the head on both sides, and it is often accompanied by a stuffy or runny nose. The patient's hands, feet, and face may swell up just before the headaches strikes, and he or she may suffer from nausea and vomiting. There may be a weight gain due to excess fluids just before the headache, and a great deal of urination and loss of the excess weight after the headache passes.

Another common type of headache is the migraine. Usually there are warning signals for this kind of headache, such as flashes or spots before the eyes. Then comes a throbbing head pain, usually on one side of the head, often followed by nausea or vomiting. A dull head pain and a generally washed-out feeling may last for a day or more afterward. Many patients find that the worst effects of the migraine can be avoided if they take a combination of aspirin and caffeine immediately at the first warning signs. Drugs such as Dilantin can also be used to prevent and control migraine.

Migraine headaches can be caused not only by allergies but also by emotional or physical stress, hormone imbalance, infections, stomach upsets, and sudden weather changes. A common nonallergic cause of migraines is a chemical called tyramine,

93

found in cheese, chocolate, and red wine. In about half the cases migraines first occur between the ages of twenty and thirty, but they can also start in early childhood or in later life. Some women who have been plagued by migraines due to hormonal causes find that they disappear at menopause; others begin to have migraines at menopause. A tendency to have migraine headaches seems to be hereditary: if the parents have them, chances are some of the children will have them too.

When headaches are caused by allergies, avoidance of the allergens can bring relief.

How Allergies Are Diagnosed and Treated

> Speak roughly to your little boy,
> And beat him when he sneezes.
> He only does it to annoy,
> Because he knows it teases.

Alice in Wonderland did not have any trouble diagnosing the cause of the sneezes the Duchess was complaining about. The air in the stuffy kitchen was filled with pepper, an irritant that can make anybody sneeze. But in real life the problem of recognizing allergies and distinguishing them from infectious diseases and reactions to irritants is often not so simple.

Picture a child who has been suffering from one "cold" after another, with a chronic cough that hangs on and on. Is he really suffering from bacterial or viral infections? Or allergies? Or perhaps a combination of both?

Many allergists say that they can often recognize a child with nasal allergies almost from the mo-

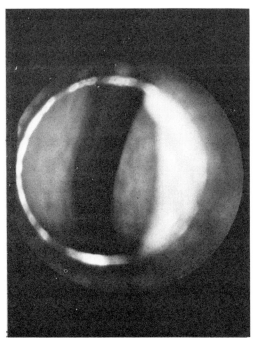

These photos were taken inside people's noses: (1) an allergic rhinitis patient; (2) a normal person.

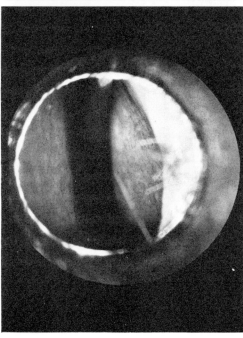

ment he walks in the door. He is pale and sallow, with puffiness around the eyes and dark smudges under them (the "allergic shiner"). His mouth may hang open, as he breathes through it instead of his clogged nose, and his teeth may be pushed out of place as a result. A look inside the child's nose reveals membranes so swollen that the air passages are almost closed. But the membranes are not red and angry-looking, as they are in an infectious disease; instead they are moist, pale, and bluish. The child may provide the final clue, giving the allergist the "allergic salute": he rubs his nose upward and outward rather than from side to side as most people do, vainly trying to ease the itching and get more air. In fact, the skin across the bridge of his nose may show a distinct horizontal crease, produced by repeated upward rubbing.

Once the presence of allergies is established, or at least strongly suspected, the next question is: Allergic to what?

Detailed questioning of the patient provides the allergist with many valuable clues. What kind of symptoms are there, when do they occur, and when are they worst? Sneezing, itching throat, and running eyes that occur only during a particular season of the year are probably an indication of allergy to the pollen of plants that bloom then, or to seasonal

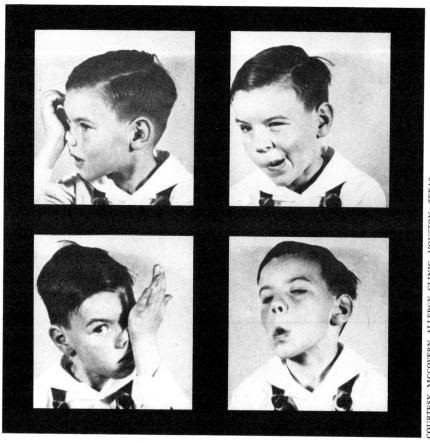

The "allergic salute."

molds, or perhaps to foods that are plentiful in that season. The same symptoms occurring all year round may indicate an allergy to dust, pets, or some food that is eaten frequently. What are the patient's habits? Are cosmetics used frequently? Is the patient a smoker? (In addition to all the other bad effects smoking can have, a sensitivity to cigarette smoke can cause asthma, and some smokers develop a contact dermatitis on the fingers that hold the cigarette.)

Tests for contact dermatitis are easy once the doctor has a hint of possible allergens. A small sample of the suspected substance or an extract of it is taped to the patient's skin and then removed after one to

The patch test.

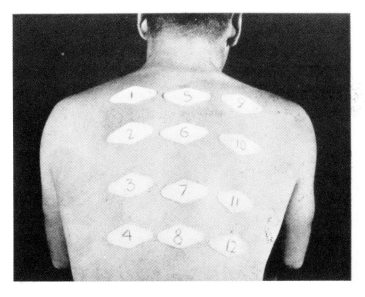

two days. (Often the substance itself is too irritating to use for testing and must first be diluted to a safe level.) If the patient is allergic to the substance, the skin beneath the sample will show an angry red patch. This kind of allergy test is called a "patch test."

Skin tests are also commonly used for types of allergies involving IgE antibody reactions. In one variation, the "scratch test," a series of scratches are made on the patient's skin (usually the inner surface of the forearm), and a solution containing a tiny bit of an allergen is placed on each one. The formation of a swelling that looks like a mosquito bite, with redness around it, indicates an allergy to the substance used. In another variation, the "intradermal test," a tiny portion of an allergen solution is injected into the skin (*not* into an artery or vein—the doctor does not want the allergen to get into the patient's bloodstream, where it might cause a serious systemic reaction).

In cases where a patient is so sensitive that even the tiny amount of allergen applied in a scratch or intradermal test might spark a serious reaction, or where he or she is suffering from a skin disorder, an indirect test can be used. Blood serum of a patient is injected into several places in the skin of a normal person. This produces a temporary allergy in the

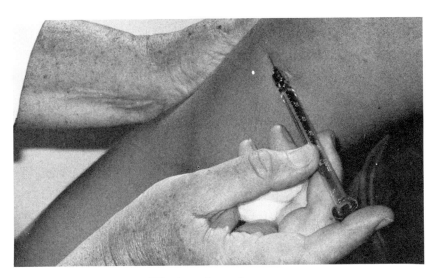

The intradermal test.

normal person's skin. Then, forty-eight hours later, the normal person is given an intradermal test at the site of the injection. This kind of indirect or "passive transfer test" can also be used to check the results of a direct skin test on the patient. However, the passive transfer test carries the danger of transmitting serum hepatitis, a serious viral disease. Careful screening of the patient's blood for hepatitis virus is necessary, and this kind of allergy test is seldom used anymore.

Skin tests for allergies are based on the fact that, even when the symptoms are in the nose, lungs, digestive tract, or some other area of the body, the allergic person usually has some of the sensitized IgE in the skin as well. Skin tests are usually fairly reliable for allergies to ragweed and other pollens, but they may not be as reliable for food and drug allergies (even when the person normally has a skin reaction after eating a particular food). The application or injection of a food allergen may give a negative reaction even when the person really is allergic to it. In such cases the person is probably allergic not to chemicals in the food itself, but to changed forms of chemicals that are produced in the body when the food is digested. Negative results are also obtained if the patient has been taking antihistamines. Or the test extract may not have been prepared or preserved properly and may not be reliable.

Sometimes a positive skin test is obtained even though the person does not show any symptoms when he or she is exposed to a substance. Such a positive test may be an indication of an allergy the patient used to have. IgE antibodies are still circulating in the blood and are attached to mast cells in the skin, but they are no longer fixed to mast cells in the shock organ, or they don't trigger the release of the mast cells' allergy-producing chemicals. Hence, the patient shows no symptoms. Sometimes a positive test may indicate a substance to which the person is becoming sensitive. It often happens that young children who have positive tests for pollen allergies, although they have never had any seasonal symptoms, develop hay fever or other seasonal allergies within two years.

Skin tests for allergies may be a long, drawn-out process. A person has only a limited amount of skin that can be scratched or injected and watched for reactions, and the doctor may not want to challenge the patient's immune system with too many allergens at once. A new type of test, developed in Sweden, may ultimately solve this problem. This test, called the radioallergosorbent technique (RAST), uses a sample of the patient's blood. Samples of thirty or more allergens are bonded to a paper disk, which is then treated with the patient's blood sample. If the patient is allergic to one or more of the allergens, the blood will contain the specific kind of IgE that reacts with that allergen. When the paper disk is washed, all the specific IgEs will remain on the paper, held in complexes with the corresponding allergens. Then the disk is treated with specially prepared radioactive antibodies against IgE, "labeled" with a radioactive isotope of iodine. These antibodies, in turn, will "label" the IgE spots on the paper, and their location can be readily determined with a gamma radiation counter. Any allergen spot on the disk that shows radioactivity indicates an allergy, and the higher the radiation count, the more specific IgE there was in the patient's blood—therefore, the greater the sensitivity to that particular allergen. The use of computers is making RAST tests faster and more accurate. A technician can perform two to three hundred RAST tests in one day, using only a drop of blood serum for each one. RAST tests have been developed for common pollens, animal danders, insect venoms, and other allergens and are expected to become increasingly useful in the years to come.

Skin tests and RAST tests cannot always solve the allergist's diagnostic problems. Food allergies are often especially difficult to pinpoint. The doctor can try several other approaches. One is having the patient try an elimination diet. After the patient has been keeping a food diary for a while, all the foods that are suspected as possible allergens are eliminated from the patient's diet to see if the symptoms disappear. If neither the patient nor the doctor has any real idea which foods to suspect, then all the most common allergenic foods, such as milk, eggs, corn, wheat, strawberries, and so forth, are eliminated. (Care must be taken to ensure that the foods that are left still provide wholesome, well-balanced nutrition.) If the symptoms clear up, then foods are gradually reintroduced, one at a time, in small and then increasing amounts, waiting at least a few days before reintroducing each new food. If the patient has no trouble with milk and eggs, but gets hives or sniffles again when wheat is reintroduced, the puzzle is probably solved.

Once the allergist has determined what the patient is allergic to, the question remains: What to do about it? Unfortunately, so far there are no real cures for allergies. But there are several approaches that can be used to control them effectively enough so that the patient can live a fairly normal life. The three main practical alternatives are: (1) avoid the allergens; (2) treat the symptoms; and (3) attempt to desensitize the patient.

If strawberries give you hives and grapefruit makes you wheeze, but no other allergens bother you, you will not find it very difficult to stay in good health by avoiding these allergens. People who are allergic to foods like milk, eggs, and wheat have a more difficult time avoiding their allergens, since they are found in so many foods that form a normal part of the diet. People sensitive to allergens in the air, such as ragweed pollen or house dust, may find it almost impossible to escape the allergen that plagues them. There are some regions of the United States that are fairly free of ragweed, and some hay fever and asthma sufferers try to vacation in such "pollen refuges" during the pollen season. They may even consider moving to another climate completely, to gain relief from their allergic symptoms. Sometimes this works. But since allergic people are often sensitive to more than one thing, the patient who moves to escape allergies may find after a time that he or she is becoming sensitive to tree, grass, or weed pollen or to other allergens that are found in the new locality.

Some relief may be gained by partial measures such as the use of an air conditioner, especially one equipped with an electrostatic filter that can trap the tiny pollen grains. Reducing the amount of allergens in the air the patient breathes can reduce the symptoms, or even bring the allergen level down below the sensitivity threshold, so that there is no reaction at all. In cases of dust allergies, in addition to using effective air conditioning, special care should be taken to houseclean, vacuum, wet-mop, and damp-dust frequently. (If possible, someone who is not allergic should do the cleaning. If the allergy patient must do it, he or she can cut down symptoms by wearing a filter mask.) The allergy patient's bedroom is especially important. Dust catchers like rugs, curtains, and knickknacks should be avoided, the mattress should be covered with a dustproof zippered cover, and the pillows should be a nonallergenic type such as Dacron, rather than feather pillows. (Foam rubber pillows used to be recommended, but they can harbor molds.)

Special hypoallergenic cosmetics are available for allergy-prone people. They are made without the usual allergen ingredients in cosmetics, such as orrisroot, certain perfumes, and coal tar dyes.

Some allergy sufferers find that their symptoms are controlled satisfactorily by drugs. Literally dozens of antihistamines and decongestants are available. Some are sold over the counter in drugstores; others must be prescribed by a physician and taken under a

Allergy patients have a wide choice of antihistamines.

doctor's supervision. Antihistamines are believed to work by competing with histamine for receptors—active spots on the surface of cells that normally react with histamine. If an antihistamine molecule is blocking the receptor, histamine molecules cannot get to it and produce their effects.

Antihistamines can have unwanted side effects, including drowsiness, blurring of vision, disturbances of the stomach and intestines, and a retention of urine. The side effects vary from drug to drug and from person to person, and the antihistamine effects of the drugs vary too. Some people find that one particular drug, such as Pyribenzamine, Chlortrimeton, or Benadryl, works best for them, while others find the same drug of little use. Sometimes an allergy patient will take a particular antihistamine successfully for years and then suddenly find that it no longer helps, while another antihistamine is effective. Often the patient must proceed by trial and error, trying one antihistamine after another until an effective one is found.

Corticosteroid hormones, natural body chemicals that are produced by the adrenal glands, can be helpful in relieving nasal congestion and opening up the bronchial tubes. But they can have serious side effects—upsetting the body's balances of water, salts, proteins, and sugar and sometimes causing stomach ulcers, depression, and high blood pressure, or leaving the body unable to cope with the extra stress of a serious infection or a surgical operation. So these powerful hormones are given under strict medical supervision and, except in cases where they are needed on a long-term basis, are used only to help tide asthma patients over the worst of a serious attack.

One of the newer antiasthma drugs, cromolyn sodium, works by keeping the antibody-antigen complex from acting on the mast cells; thus it blocks the release of histamine and other mediator chemicals. In addition to its value in preventing asthma attacks, some allergists believe that cromolyn sodium may be effective in hay fever as well. (In asthma the drug is taken by bronchial inhalation, and in hay fever by nasal inhalation.)

Many allergists believe that the best way currently available to control allergies is through a series of desensitization injections. An extract containing a tiny dose of the allergen or allergens to which the patient is sensitive is injected. Each week the injection is repeated, with gradually increasing doses, carefully controlled so that the patient will not have a bad reaction. The higher the dose of injected allergen can be raised, the better able the patient will be to tolerate the allergen in the environment. This is not a quick treatment by any means. It may be months

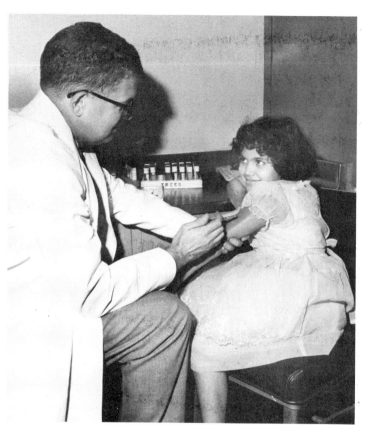

Injection treatments can bring relief to many allergy sufferers.

before relief is obtained, and several years before symptoms are reduced to a minimum. The patient never *completely* loses sensitivity to the pollen or other allergen, but he or she is able to live with it in reasonable comfort. (Some doctors prefer to use the term *hyposensitization*, meaning "a little sensitivity," rather than *desensitization*, which implies that the sensitivity will be completely gone.) Injection treatments are not effective for all types of allergies; they work best for ragweed pollen hay fever.

It may seem hard to believe that injecting an allergen—which is a dangerous poison for an allergy patient—can actually build up tolerance to the allergen instead of provoking an allergic attack. Of course, the allergen is entering the body in a different way—injected into the skin instead of inhaled or eaten—but why does it not stimulate the IgE system? And how can it provide protection against future attacks? Actually, when an allergen is injected into the skin, it does stimulate the IgE system, especially at first, but such tiny doses are used that the reaction is not serious. At the same time, it is believed, the injected antigen stimulates the formation of a different kind of antibody—the IgG antibodies that normally battle against foreign invaders. Once enough IgG antibodies are formed, they act as blocking antibodies, tying up any allergen molecules that enter the body in the usual way and preventing the sensitized IgE from getting to them. As the doses of allergen are increased, eventually a point is reached where the body contains more sensitized IgG (blocking antibodies) than IgE, and then the person can tolerate an exposure to the allergen without developing allergic symptoms. There is evidence that a series of desensitization injections can also gradually lower the amount of IgE that the body produces and make the mast cells less sensitive to the action of the IgE-antigen complexes, but how these effects are produced is not yet known.

Desensitization injections as they are usually given are not an ideal treatment. In order to gain relief, the patient must invest a great deal of time and effort, seeing the doctor, for example, every week or two for years. Some people are afraid of injections. (We know a doctor who suffers each fall from the miseries of hay fever. When asked why he never took a series of desensitization injections—which he could have received right in his own office from his partner—he shrugged and said, "I don't like shots.")

Allergists have been trying a number of ways to make the treatment easier and more effective. One method that was popular a few years ago was the "one-shot" treatment. Instead of preparing the allergen in a water extract, which is immediately absorbed into the body, it was prepared in the form of an oil emulsion. This mixture, when injected into the skin, breaks down very, very slowly, releasing tiny amounts of the allergen at a time. So an entire year's dose of allergen could be given in just one, or perhaps two or three injections, instead of fifty or so.

This method was first developed by Dr. Mary Loveless of Cornell University Medical College, and it gave very good results for many patients. But as it began to be used more widely, serious problems showed up. If the oil emulsion was not prepared exactly right, it might break down too quickly, releasing a dangerously large dose of the allergen into the patient's body at one time. In some people, the mineral oil used for the emulsion formed an annoying lump under the skin, which did not go away; sometimes abscesses formed at the site of the injection. And then experiments on animals indicated that the injected mineral oil might be a possible cause of cancer! Though the animal tests may not be an indication of danger for humans, they do call for caution in using the technique until more is known.

A somewhat similar but safer "one-shot" treatment may be provided by new techniques of microencapsulation, which are being developed to deliver controlled amounts of drugs, hormones, and other chemicals into the body. The chemicals are enclosed in tiny packets (microcapsules), which may break down gradually to release their contents over a period of many months, or may be "leaky" enough to permit some body chemicals to pass freely in and out of the microcapsule, while the drugs are firmly held inside.

Some researchers are working on the idea of using pure chemical antigens for desensitization injections, instead of extracts from whole pollen grains, which are a mixture of many chemicals. Several antigens that have already been isolated from ragweed pollen are believed to be the cause of most rag-

Animals are used in some allergy research. This dog has been made allergic by a passive transfer of antibodies.

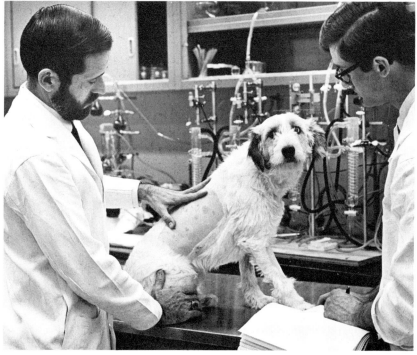

weed allergies. Researchers hope that injections of these pure allergens will provide more effective protection and fewer side effects.

Experimental preparations made from chemically modified allergens are also being tried. For example, treatment with formaldehyde—a substance commonly used to preserve biological specimens— changes pollen antigens chemically so that they become inactive but can still stimulate the production of antibodies. It is hoped that by using such changed allergens—called "allergoids"—much higher doses can be used without danger of allergic reactions, and tolerance can be built up faster, with fewer injections.

Meanwhile, as scientists gain more knowledge of how allergic reactions work, some exciting advances in applying this knowledge are being made.

Frontiers of Allergy Research

We are in the midst of a biological revolution. Scientists are studying the chemical reactions of life and learning more and more about them. Biochemists and molecular biologists now have the tools and techniques for determining the chemical structures of very complicated molecules such as proteins. They know how to find the active spots on the surface of cells that serve as receptors for hormones and other chemical messengers, and to study how the cell receptors interact with these chemicals. The new tools, techniques, and discoveries are helping allergy researchers to gain further insights into how allergic reactions occur and what can be done to prevent them.

The allergy research described in this chapter is only a small sampling of the many exciting and promising studies that may help to bring relief to allergy sufferers. All over the world, many researchers are working on studies in these and other areas. Some of the leads that seem promising today may not prove out after all; other areas may yield new fruitful approaches and unexpected breakthroughs.

Lawrence Goodfriend, a biochemist at McGill University in Montreal, has been working out the chemical structure of ragweed pollen antigens. The first to be worked out completely, an antigen called Ra5, turned out to have a very rigid three-dimensional structure. This kind of structure is just what would be expected for an allergen, since its characteristic shape would make it easily recognizable to antibody-forming cells. Dr. Goodfriend hopes that a knowledge of the structure of allergens will help in understanding exactly what happens chemically when an allergen molecule reacts with an IgE-producing cell.

David Katz and his colleagues at Harvard Medical School are working on ways to switch off the antibody-forming cells that produce allergies to penicillin and other allergens. Their idea is to attach an allergen to a "carrier" protein and give small, repeated doses of the complex. The theory is that the complex would be recognized by the two different kinds of lymphocytes—the B-cells that make the antibodies and the T-cells that help them to function. The B-cells would recognize the antigen part of the complex, and the T-cells would recognize the carrier part. By getting just the right combination, the researchers hoped to be able to switch off the B-cells, so that antibodies would not be formed. Recent experiments on rats indicate that they are on the right track. The researchers linked a form of penicillin, benzylpenicilloyl, with an artificial protein, D-GL, formed from just two amino acids—glutamic acid and lysine. Injections of this complex protected the rats from penicillin allergy for at least six months.

Other allergy researchers are studying the mast cells and the mediator chemicals they secrete, trying to find ways of blocking the secretion or interaction of these chemicals.

K. Frank Austen and his colleagues at Harvard Medical School and Robert B. Brigham Hospital in Boston wondered why the tears, nasal mucus, and other fluids produced in allergic reactions contain an unusually large number of a particular kind of white blood cells called eosinophils. (Testing for eosinophils is one of the tests some allergists use to establish the presence of allergies, but for a long time no one knew what role they play.) Dr. Austen discovered that the eosinophils are attracted by a substance secreted by the mast cells. He named this secretion ECF-A, or eosinophil chemotactic factor of anaphylaxis. ("Chemotactic" is a term referring to a chemical that produces movement by cells.) He has determined the chemical structure of ECF-A and synthesized (or artificially reproduced) it in the laboratory.

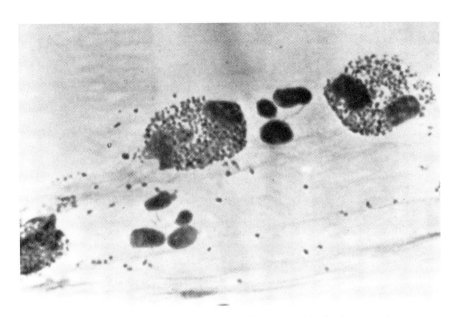

Eosinophils are shown in this highly magnified picture of a nasal smear.

Dr. Austen and his associates have also been studying SRS-A ("slow-reacting substance of anaphylaxis"), a chemical mediator that plays an important role in producing the symptoms of asthma. Knowledge of part of the structure of this chemical suggested looking for some enzymes that might destroy it. Finally the researchers found one, an enzyme called arylsulfatase. This enzyme is found in eosinophils. Apparently ECF-A and the eosinophils that it summons are one of the body's own mechanisms for limiting the destructive effects of allergic reactions—by destroying the mediator chemical.

The discovery of IgE and the role it plays was probably the most important landmark achievement in modern allergy research. Immunologist Robert Hamburger at the University of California, San Diego, has been investigating the structure of this antibody, how it differs from the other major classes of antibodies, and how it interacts with the mast cells. In one intriguing study, Dr. Hamburger had one of his colleagues synthesize parts of the IgE molecule from the "tail" of the Y, the part that binds to the mast cells. When he had a collection of small peptides (short amino acid chains) to work with, Dr. Hamburger recruited volunteers: himself, his wife and two daughters, and colleagues, one of whom was extremely allergic to guinea pigs. Using a passive transfer test, he sensitized all the volunteers to guinea pig allergen, injected a dose of one of the peptides, and then injected a dose of guinea pig extract. With some of the peptides tested, or without any treatment at all, large red wheals appeared on the skin of the sensitized volunteers. But one peptide consisting of five amino acids (a pentapeptide) reduced the allergic reactions by as much as 80 to 90 percent.

Dr. Hamburger believes that the pentapeptide works by binding to the receptor sites of the mast

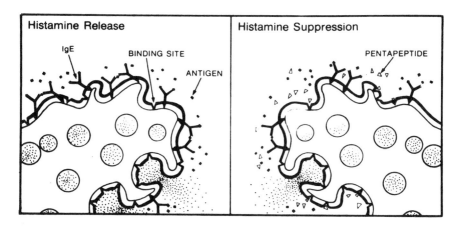

| Histamine Release | Histamine Suppression |

Robert Hamburger's pentapeptide fits into the IgE bonding sites and thus prevents allergens from sparking the histamine reaction.

cells, preventing the IgE molecules from attaching themselves and forming the allergen bridges that stimulate the release of histamine. He hopes to be able to modify the pentapeptide molecule so that it will work even better, binding more firmly to the mast cell receptors and competing more effectively with the IgE molecules. If the pentapeptide is to become a practical treatment for allergies, another necessary improvement will be a means of packaging it so that it can be taken in pill form rather than by injections, without being broken down by the digestive juices in the stomach.

Experiments such as these are still in the stage of laboratory tests, and some of the findings have not yet been confirmed by other researchers. But a growing knowledge of the chemistry of allergies may ultimately yield true cures for allergic diseases.

For Further Information

Some helpful pamphlets about various aspects of allergies can be obtained by writing to:

Allergy Foundation of America
801 Second Avenue
New York, N.Y. 10017

and

Information Office
National Institute of Allergy and
Infectious Diseases
National Institutes of Health
Bethesda, Maryland 20014

Index

Page references in *italics* indicate illustrations.